POMPOMANIA

how to make over 20 characterful pompoms

Christine Leech

Photography by
Joanna Henderson

DAVID & CHARLES

www.davidandcharles.com

A DAVID AND CHARLES BOOK
© David and Charles, Ltd 2024

David and Charles is an imprint of David and Charles, Ltd, Suite A, Tourism House, Pynes Hill, Exeter, EX2 5WS

Text and Layout © Christine Leech 2024
Photography (excluding images on pages 64–7) © Joanna Henderson 2024

First published in 2016 by Quadrille, an imprint of Hardie Grant UK Ltd
This edition first published in 2024

Names of manufacturers and product ranges are provided for the information of readers, with no intention to infringe copyright or trademarks.

A catalogue record for this book is available from the British Library.

ISBN-13: 9781446314357 hardback
ISBN-13: 9781446314371 EPUB
ISBN-13: 9781446314364 PDF

This book has been printed on paper from approved suppliers and made from pulp from sustainable sources.

10 9 8 7 6 5 4 3 2 1

Printed in China through Asia Pacific Offset for David and Charles, Ltd, Suite A, Tourism House, Pynes Hill, Exeter, EX2 5WS

MIX
Paper | Supporting responsible forestry
FSC® C136333
www.fsc.org

David and Charles publishes high-quality books on a wide range of subjects.
For more information visit www.davidandcharles.com.

Share your makes with us on social media using #dandcbooks and follow us on Facebook and Instagram by searching for @dandcbooks.

Layout of the digital edition of this book may vary depending on reader hardware and display settings.

CONTENTS

INTRODUCTION

The most common refrain heard when I told people I was writing a book on pompoms was 'Oh, I used to make those as a child.' And so did I. I spent hours winding yarn onto basic cardboard pompom makers cut from cereal packets, then turning the results into fluffy chicks or monsters with big googly eyes. When I was asked to write this book, I was a little apprehensive about the time it can take to make a pompom and what exactly you might do with those simple spheres. I soon learnt that the humble cardboard maker has been replaced by more efficient plastic contraptions for speedy pompom making and that there are hundreds of things that you can do with a pompom.

While some projects in this book are simple and require basic pompom-making techniques, others are more complex and involve a bit of brain power... but the results are amazing. Once you have got your head around the way a pattern is created within a pompom, there is no end to what you can create. The most exciting moment in pompom making comes when you cut through all the wraps of yarn and the pattern you hope you have created begins to reveal itself. There were many experiments when planning these projects, but even though some did not turn out just the way I expected, they all had a certain charm. Even the ones I initially considered a failure turned out pretty much okay after a hard trim with some sharp scissors. As in life, a good haircut can work wonders.

In this book I have used an acrylic DK-weight yarn from a company called Stylecraft (who were kind enough to give me many balls of yarn for experimentation). I recommend you also use a similar DK-weight yarn so that the number of wraps of each colour yarn are consistent with the instructions given. The colours mentioned in the instructions are specific to Stylecraft but it is easy to swap in colours based on whatever yarn you have to hand. When choosing yarns for your pompom making, inexpensive acrylic DK-weight yarns work best as they fluff up nicely when trimmed. Using an aran-weight or bulky yarn does mean less winding to fill the pompom maker, which makes for a speedier pom, but may give a less defined pattern. Some of the weirder and more wonderful yarns with sequins and fluffy bits make incredible pompoms, so have fun and try lots of different types.

As I sit at my desk writing this introduction, surrounded by all the projects I made for this book, I am struck by how versatile the humble pompom can be. When asked to write this book, never in my wildest dreams did I imagine I would be able to show you how to make pompoms in the shape of sushi!

Happy Pompoming!

Christine

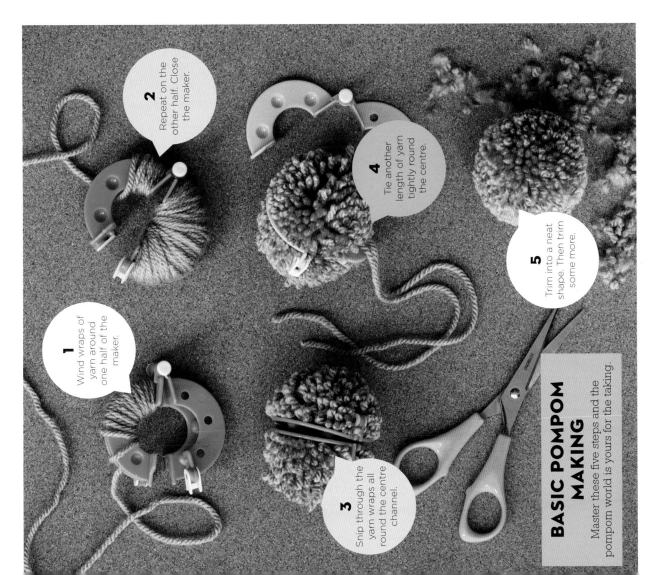

BASIC POMPOM MAKING

Master these five steps and the pompom world is yours for the taking.

1 Wind wraps of yarn around one half of the maker.

2 Repeat on the other half. Close the maker.

3 Snip through the yarn wraps all round the centre channel.

4 Tie another length of yarn tightly round the centre.

5 Trim into a neat shape. Then trim some more.

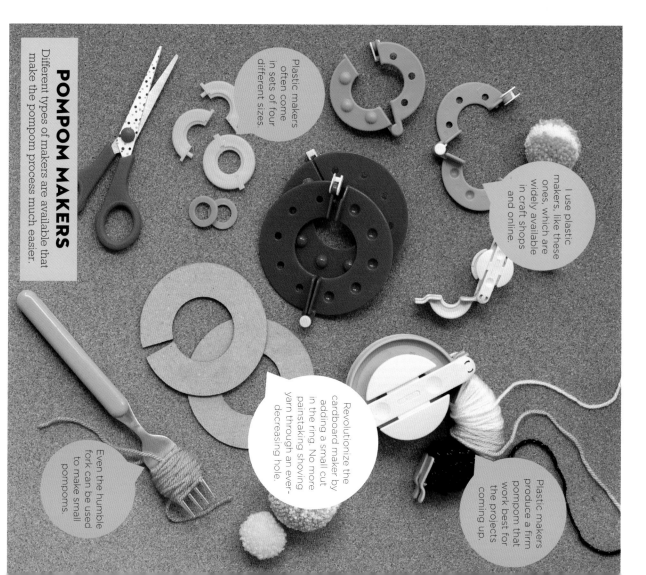

POMPOM MAKERS

Different types of makers are available that make the pompom process much easier.

Plastic makers often come in sets of four different sizes.

I use plastic makers, like these ones, which are widely available in craft shops and online.

Revolutionize the cardboard maker by adding a small cut in the ring. No more painstaking shoving yarn through an ever-decreasing hole.

Even the humble fork can be used to make small pompoms.

Plastic makers produce a firm pompom that work best for the projects coming up.

FORK POMPOMS

You can buy tiny pompom makers, but they are fiddly to use and easy to lose. Forks are the perfect size to make smaller pompoms. Plus, if you are ever at a restaurant with a ball of yarn, well, there's your after-dinner entertainment right there.

1

Cut a length of yarn to approximately 15cm (6 in). Place it between middle tines of a fork.

2

Wind yarn round fork 50 times, making sure cut end does not get caught up in wraps.

3

Once finished winding, use two cut ends to gather wraps tightly together. Tie into a knot.

4

If you find it tricky to pull yarn bundle tight, slip it off tines, gather and tie another knot.

5

Snip through each side of yarn bundle to release yarn strands.

6

Trim pompom with scissors into a neat, round shape. Keep brushing the strands to reveal any stray bits.

POMPOM PERFECTION

1 I find it easier to start wrapping yarn in the centre of a maker; it is less fiddly than trying to start at one end. With the fingers of one hand, hold the cut end of the yarn in place on the maker. Wind the yarn around the maker, catching the cut end under the wraps to hold it in place. If the instructions require you to wrap from one end, start in the centre then slide the yarn to the side once it is secure. Alternatively, tie the yarn on with a knot.

2 Wind the yarn evenly across the maker with a constant tension. It is easy to wind too much yarn in the centre of the maker halves and then the makers do not close properly. There is nothing worse than having your makers fly open after you have cut through all the wool and hundreds of strands of wool go falling to the floor. Believe me, I know!

3 Do not wrap the yarn round the maker too tightly as it is then harder to cut later. When you have completed a pompom, take a good pair of sharp scissors, insert the tip of the blades between the two halves of the maker and snip.

4 After you have cut open your pompom, you need to tie another piece of yarn round the centre to stop all the bits falling out. Rather than tying a double knot straight away, tie one knot, wrap the yarn back on itself, pull tightly, then tie a double knot for a much tighter pompom.

5 Keep trimming. I learnt a lot making the pompoms for this book. My main realization was that trimming is key! I went back to my basket of reject pompoms and realized that if I had spent more time with the scissors, carefully trimming round and round the pom I thought was a no-no, it would actually have been a yes-yes. Rolling the pompom between your hands moves the strands and shows up any bits that need a snip. Do this periodically as you trim for the perfect finish.

6 Cheat a little. There are some projects in this book that require lots of colour changes and small wraps of yarn. Once you have completed a project and trimmed the pompom, do not be afraid to pull out strands that make your pattern look uneven or even add ones in where there is a hole. Thread a large darning needle with the required colour and 'sew' it through the pompom in the necessary place, then trim. This method works well when adding eyes and highlights to faces, such as the dog on pages 88–91.

7 Use the tip of a darning needle or the point of some scissors to move individual strands of yarn around. As pompoms are tied so tightly, when you move a strand it tends to stay in place. This is great for projects like the Dia de Muertos skull on pages 84–7, ensuring the colours for his eyes and teeth are in the right place.

TIP

Trim, trim and then trim some more. The more you trim a pompom, the neater and more obvious the pattern you have added inside it becomes. Though as with hair, the wild, tousled look sometimes works too!

LOOPED POMPOMS

Another fork method for making pompoms, but this time a sweet looped variety. Combining traditional fluffy pompoms with these loopy ones looks great on sweaters, socks, necklaces or cushions. There is not much that can't be improved by the addition of a pompom.

1
Cut a 15cm (6 in) length of yarn. Place it between middle tines of a fork.

2
Take ball of yarn and begin weaving strand from ball between tines, over and under each one.

3
Work back and forth across tines until fork is completely full.

4
Using 15cm (6 in) length of yarn, gather woven yarn on tines together. Tie tightly into a knot.

5
To tighten knot gradually, slide woven yarn off of fork. Tighten as you go, then tie in a double knot.

6
Rearrange loops to neaten pompom and form a neat, round sphere.

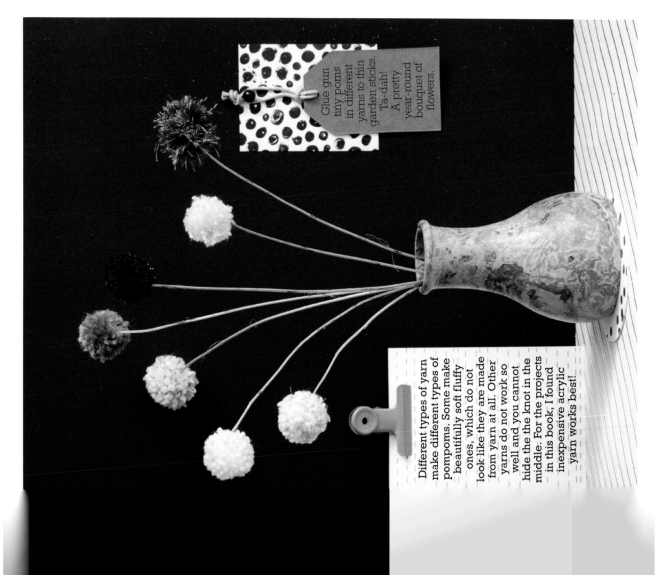

Glue gun tiny poms in different yarns to thin garden sticks. Ta-dah! A pretty year-round bouquet of flowers.

Different types of yarn make different types of pompoms. Some make beautifully soft fluffy ones, which do not look like they are made from yarn at all. Other yarns do not work so well and you cannot hide the the knot in the middle. For the projects in this book, I found inexpensive acrylic yarn works best!

MULTIPLE POMPOMS

Sometimes you need a lot of pompoms… and you need them fast! For those emergency pompom moments, this method of making multiple poms is really handy.

1

Using an A5 notebook or a piece of card measuring approximately 21cm (8¼ in) in length, wrap yarn around card 70 times.

2

Slide the skein of yarn from the notebook or piece of card.

3

Starting 3cm (1¾ in) from end, tie a length of yarn around the skein in 6cm (2⅜ in) intervals, finishing 3cm (1¾ in) from end.

4

Using scissors, cut the skein into four. Cut through the loops of two pompoms at either end.

5

Shake the pompoms. Then trim. How much yarn you trim determines how neat your pompoms look (and how small they become).

TIP

If you want to make even more pompoms in one go, simply use a larger notebook or piece of card. You could also use a chair back or an obliging friend's pair of arms to wind the yarn round.

POMPOM LAMPSHADES

Use multiple pompoms to decorate old lampshades that have seen better days. Remove the fabric coverings and spray the frames with black paint. Use a glue gun to stick different shapes and colours of pompoms in place. For safety, remember to use a low-emissions light bulb though.

NO-HASSLE TASSELS

A great partner to the pompom is the tassel. These are super-quick and can be made in any size and shade. I have made some small ones to give my Dala horse a brightly coloured mane, but they are also great added to jewellery, bag charms, garlands and chandeliers.

1

Cut a rectangle of card to height you want finished tassel to be.
Cut a length of yarn to approximately 15cm (6 in).
Lay it alongside card.

2

Wrap yarn around card and over the cut length of yarn. The more wraps, the plumper the tassel. These mini ones are made with 25 wraps of yarn.

3

When complete, use cut piece of yarn to tie a double knot tightly around yarn bundle. Slide yarn bundle off of piece of card.

4

Tie another cut length of yarn around yarn bundle, approximately one quarter of way down from tied end.

5

Cut bottom edge of bundle to release strands of yarn. Trim to neaten.
Use yarn tails or a glue gun to fix tassel in place.

TIP

For multi-coloured tassels, wrap two or three different yarns at the same time. For tassels with a different coloured core, first wrap one colour then cover with another. For stripey tassels, wrap blocks of different colours next to each other.

ONE-COLOUR POMPOMS

RAINCLOUD MOBILE

I love a cloud craft project and try to get one into every book I write. Clouds and pompoms are a match made in weather heaven, so when I saw Anna Thomas's work of art, I had to have a go at making a more simple version.

For the cloud:
DK-weight acrylic yarn in the following colours: silver, parma violet, sunshine

For the raindrops:
DK-weight acrylic yarn in the following colours: sherbert, royal, atlantis, white, midnight, bluebell, turquoise, cloud blue, emperor, aster

3.5cm (1⅜ in), 5.5cm (2⅛ in), 9cm (3½ in) and 11.5cm (4½ in) diameter pompom makers

Darning needle

Make the following pompoms:
1 x 11.5cm (4½ in) in a mixture of silver and parma violet
1 x 9cm (3½ in) in parma violet
1 x 9cm (3½ in) in silver
1 x 5.5cm (2⅛ in) in silver
1 x 5.5cm (2⅛ in) in parma violet
1 x 3.5cm (1⅜ in) in silver
1 x 5.5cm (2⅛ in) in sunshine

TO MAKE THE RAINCLOUD

1

Thread darning needle with yarn tails and use to attach smaller pompoms to larger. Sew until all poms are firmly joined.

2

Add smallest 3.5cm (1⅜ in) pompom underneath 11.5cm (4½ in) one. Then add two 9cm (3½ in) pompoms either side.

3

Fix two 5.5cm (2⅛ in) pompoms in between the 9cm (3½ in) ones to make a cloud shape.

4

Fix 5.5cm (2⅛ in) sun pompom to back of cloud, so sun appears to be just peeking over cloud.

CONTINUED...

TO MAKE THE RAINDROPS

Make three 5.5cm (2⅛in) pompoms in atlantis, turquoise, and aster, then make 3.5cm (1⅜in) pompoms from the rest of the colours. When cutting the yarn, make sure you leave long tails for tying the raindrop pompoms to the cloud.

1

Remove pompom from maker. Start trimming pompom into a cone shape.

2

Cut into pompom at an angle towards yarn tails used to tie pom together.

3

Trim all around yarn tails to make a neat cone-shaped pompom.

4

Trim bottom of pompom into a neat round shape. Keep trimming until you are happy with the shape.

5

Trim away one yarn tail. Thread darning needle with remaining tail and attach it to base of cloud.

TIP

When trimming your pompoms, keep brushing the yarn between cuts to keep the shape neat.

POMSAI TREES

There is something very zen and calming about these pomsai trees. They make great deskmates and do not require quite as much maintenance as their living bonsai counterparts.

Make a selection of pompoms in different sizes and shades of green. For the larger tree, I made 1 x 7cm (2¾ in), 2 x 5.5cm (2⅛ in), 5 x 3.5cm (1⅜ in) pompoms, and 4 x small ones made on a fork (see page 7). For the smaller tree, I made 2 x 5.5cm (2⅛ in) pompoms, 5 x 3.5cm (1⅜ in) and 2 x small ones made on a fork. Trim them all so they are compact and spherical.

To fix the pompoms to the twig trunk:

1 Luckily I had these beautiful stones from a beach in Croatia, where many had natural holes, which makes them a perfect stand for the pomsai. If you can find similar pebbles, then brilliant. If not, a lump of air-dry modelling clay works too.

2 Trim your twig to about 12cm (4¾ in) high, then form the clay into a pebble shape and insert the twig. Make sure the pebble shape has a stable base to stand on and the twig remains upright.

3 As with real bonsai, try to visualize what the final tree will look like. Begin with the largest pompoms and glue gun one to the trunk. Working your way around the tree, keep adding further pompoms until it looks pleasing from all angles.

For the leaves:
DK-weight acrylic yarn in the following colours: greengage and khaki

3.5cm (1⅜ in), 5.5cm (2⅛ in) and 7cm (2¾ in) diameter pompom makers

Fork

Twigs from the garden or park (forked ones make for a more realistic tree)

Glue gun

Pebble with a hole in or lump of air-dry modelling clay

FOOTSTOOL

This footstool never fails to raise a smile from visitors to my house.

A great way of using up scraps of yarn, there is everything from chunky aran to fluffy angora and cotton DK here. Choose a range of colours; I went for a mix of neutral shade, grey, beige and white to allow the brighter accents of pink, orange and turquoise to stand out.

1 Make lots of pompoms in various sizes and colours. For this footstool, I made 100 pompoms! Most are one colour, but for some I wound two or three shades together for a multi-coloured effect. To do this, hold all the yarns together as you wind them onto the maker. Leave long yarn tails when tying the pompoms as these are used to sew them to the footstool.

2 Measure the padded part of your footstool.

3 Depending on the shape of your stool, cut a circle or square from stretchy fabric using this measurement. Thread the darning needle with ribbon, then sew a running stitch all round the edge. Leave a long length of ribbon at the beginning and end.

4 Place the fabric over the stool pad and gather it on the underside by pulling the ribbon ends. Once it is fitting snugly, knot the ribbon.

5 To sew the pompoms to the fabric, thread the darning needle with the yarn tail of one pompom then stitch it securely in place anywhere on the cover. Repeat with the second tail. Tie the tails together and trim.

6 Repeat with the remaining pompoms until the fabric is covered. Vary sizes so the small pompoms fill the gaps between the large ones.

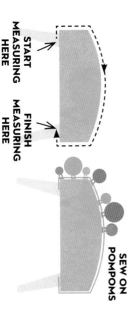

START MEASURING HERE

FINISH MEASURING HERE

SEW ON POMPOMS

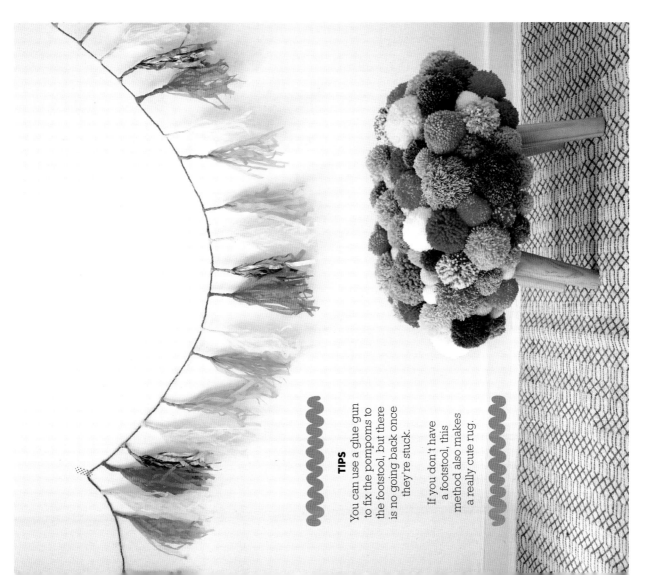

TIPS

You can use a glue gun to fix the pompoms to the footstool, but there is no going back once they're stuck.

If you don't have a footstool, this method also makes a really cute rug.

GIANT GARLAND

This garland uses one whole ball of yarn per pompom. Fortunately you do not need to wind the yarn onto a pompom maker… because that would take forever! You simply use the ball of yarn as is.

For the pompoms:
1 ball of aran-weight acrylic yarn in the following colours: spice, teal, bluebell, aspen, fondant

Scissors

2 metres (2 yards) gold ribbon, plus extra ribbons for decoration

TIP

This garland is shown above an unlit fireplace for display purposes only. Acrylic yarn and an open fire are never a good mix!

1

Wrap a 50cm (20 in) length of yarn around centre of ball. Tie tightly. Wrap and tie again, this time with a double knot.

2

Cut through loops of yarn on one side. There will be really small loops in centre of the ball, so make sure you snip all of them.

3

The ball of yarn now looks like a giant tassel. Cut through loops on other side. Shake ball to leave a messy mass of yarn.

4

Trim any long strands so ball looks pompom-like. Keep ties round centre separate. Use ties to fix pompoms to ribbon.

PAJAKI CHANDELIER

This pompom-adorned chandelier is based on a traditional Polish decoration called a pajaki, which are normally made from coloured paper and straws.

For the pompoms and tassels:
DK-weight acrylic yarn in the following colours: citron, sunshine, twilight, pearl, aspen, meadow, sunshine, green

3.5cm (1⅜ in) and 5.5cm (2⅛ in) diameter pompom makers

Scissors

Fork

Gold embroidery thread

Inside ring of a 25cm (9¾ in) diameter wooden embroidery hoop

Washi tape

5 metres (5 yards) gold cord

Darning needle

Glue gun

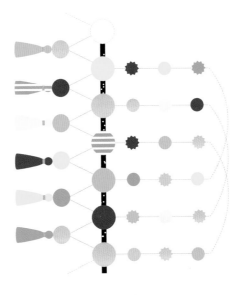

Using all the yarn colours, make 6 x 3.5cm (1⅜ in) pompoms, 6 x 5.5cm (2⅛ in) pompoms, 9 small fork pompoms (see page 7), 9 looped fork pompoms (see page 10), and 6 tassels (see page 15). To make the tassels use a postcard-sized piece of card, measuring 15cm x 10cm (6 in x 4¼ in). Wrap the yarn 20 times around the card and then use gold embroidery thread to fasten the tassel.

These pompoms and tassels are threaded onto gold cord in the next steps. The diagram above shows the different colours and the order in which I placed them to create the chandelier shown opposite.

1 Cover the outside edge of the embroidery hoop with washi tape.

2 Cut three 70cm (27½ in) lengths and six 40cm (15¾ in) lengths of gold cord.

CONTINUED...

3

Thread darning needle with 70cm (27½ in) cord. Pass through three small and looped poms alternately.

4

Repeat with two more cord lengths, plus six more small and looped poms. Mix up the colours.

5

Thread darning needle with 40cm (15¾ in) cord. Pass through tassel, then through 3.5cm (1⅜ in) pom.

6

Using glue gun, fix 5.5cm (2⅛ in) poms to hoop, each spaced equally apart.

7

Tie one end of a 70cm (27½ in) cord behind one pom on hoop. Tie other end behind opposite pom.

8

Repeat with remaining cord lengths. Hang from a hook to work comfortably on next step.

9

Using glue gun, fix each 40cm (15¾ in) cord to hoop so tassel hangs between poms on hoop.

10

Separate cords so there is a 'V' shape between each pompom. Trim away any untidy ends.

MULTI-COLOUR POMPOMS

UNDERSTANDING POM-STRUCTION

Now you have mastered the simple, single-colour pompom, it is time to tackle multi-coloured poms. Multi-coloured pompoms can be as straightforward as making half in one shade and the other half in a different shade.

More complex multi-coloured pompoms – where a design is added into the pompom itself by cleverly winding layers of colours in strategic positions – can include stripes, spots, hearts, flowers and even faces.

Before I explain how to make these trickier multi-coloured pompoms, I need to reiterate one thing. It's back to The Most Important Fact Ever When Making a Pompom: you need to wind yarn over both parts of the pompom maker. Too many times I have had to tell people that, because they have only used one of the hinged parts of their maker, they are never going to be able to complete their pompom. It has led to tears.

MEET YOUR MAKER

It is crucial to understand your pompom maker. Think of the maker as being divided into two halves, with one half being the front and the other the back.

For a pompom that is the same pattern all over (like the raspberry ripple ice cream scoop on page 71) or with an identical front and back (like the California roll sushi on page 58), then you wind the same pattern of yarns on both halves of the maker.

If you are making a pompom with a design on the front (like the heart on page 79), then you wind the pattern on one maker (the front) and fill the other maker (the back) with a single colour to complete the pompom.

If you are making a complex character pompom (like the birdie on pages 92–5) then the front maker is used to create the face and the back maker to create the back of his head.

FRONT HALF   **BACK HALF**

ABBREVIATIONS

F   Front half of maker
B   Back half of maker
LHE   Left-hand edge
RHE   Right-hand edge

IT'S ALL ABOUT SYMMETRY

When I first experimented with pompom making, I was not sure I would ever make anything more complex than a two-colour stripey pompom. But as I worked out how a pompom is formed on the maker, I began to understand what happens when I wind coloured yarns in different ways. It's all about symmetry.

When completing a pompom, as you cut the yarn around the middle of the maker, the pompom divides at that cut and you have exactly the same pattern on the left-hand and right-hand sides. Once you have comprehended this, you can start making patterns and shapes inside the pompoms.

FIRST AND LAST

As a pompom is spherical, the first wrapping of yarn on the front half of the maker ends up being the centre front of the pompom (for example, the beak of the bird or the central line of the heart).

The last wrapping will be the place where the front half joins the back half. Because of this fact, you often wind half as many wraps of yarn in these two places as they double in quantity when you remove the maker.

PUTTING PATTERN INTO A POMPOM

Before making a pompom, I first work out the design. Here are the steps I took when planning the birdie. He is nicely symmetrical, a good example to explain the principles of designing a pompom.

1 First I made a sketch of what I wanted the design – in this case, the birdie – to look like.

2 Starting with his head, I found the line of symmetry running down through his beak. This is the centre front of the pompom. The first wraps of yarn will make his beak.

FRONT HALF

BACK HALF

3 This is what the design looks like drawn as a template, showing the different colour wraps and layers of yarn.

4 If you follow the template or instructions, the actual pompom looks like this before it's removed from the maker.

CHEAT A LITTLE

There are some projects in this book that require lots of colour changes and small wraps of yarn. When you have completed a project and trimmed the pompom, do not be afraid to pull out any coloured strands that make your pompom look uneven. Equally, you can add extra strands of yarn anywhere there is a gap.

Thread a darning needle with the required colour yarn. Stitch it through the pompom in the exact spot, then trim. This method works well when adding eyes and highlights to faces (like the emoji-poms on pages 80–3).

You can also use the point of a darning needle or the tip of some scissors to move individual strands around within the pompom. This works well for projects like the sushi on pages 56–9 and the Dia de Muertos skull on pages 84–7, making sure all the colours sit in the right place.

WORKING THE WEDGE

A wedge is a very useful shape to master when it comes to making patterned pompoms, as it allows you to make shapes like spots, hearts, noses and mouths.

BUILDING A WEDGE

Instead of placing each winding of yarn adjacent to the previous wraps in a flat layer, a wedge is built up so the yarn is higher on one side or in the centre.

Begin by winding a base layer of yarn, working from left to right and then work back and forth across the maker. However, each time you reach the left-hand edge, work slightly fewer wraps. In doing this, you will have more wraps of yarn at the right-hand edge than the left.

When shown on a template, a wedge looks like this...

After you have wound the 20 wraps of blue yarn to build up the wedge, then wind the second colour yarn across the rest of the maker, bringing the second yarn up to the same level as the wedge in the first yarn. The white dotted line indicates the level of this first layer of yarn wraps.

To make a spot or a circle make a wedge that is wider in the centre than it is at the two sides.

On the pompom maker, a wedge looks like this. One side is noticeably fuller than the other, with more wraps of yarn.

In the finished pompom, a wedge looks like this. It is easy to tease this shape into neat, straight lines while trimming.

GO-GO GARLAND

These bold pompoms make a stylish garland. The addition of wooden beads help it hang nicely. Wind the front and back halves of the maker with different shades of yarns to create multi-coloured pompoms.

For the pompoms:
DK-weight acrylic yarn in: shrimp, soft peach, sherbet, stone mixed with metallic gold (I used Anchor Artiste Metallic in gold)

5.5cm (2⅛in) diameter pompom maker

Scissors

16 wooden beads, 20mm (¾in) in diameter

1 metre (1 yard) leather thonging

TIP
Sparkly gold yarn is too thin for pompom making. Mix it with a similar coloured yarn for the same effect.

1 Make one pompom in each colour combination shown below. On a 5.5cm (2⅛ in) maker, wind approximately 220 wraps to fill each half.

2 Thread the pompoms onto the leather. Gently squeeze a pompom between your fingers and thumb around the centre. You should feel it 'gives' more in one place. Thread the leather through the pompom at this point (where a hole is left when the pompom is tied). Using a large darning needle and thicker yarn or ribbon you can pull out several strands. I find it easier to place the leather thonging end between the arms of a kirby grip and sellotape in place.

3 Thread the pompoms and wooden beads alternately onto the leather thonging until you have completed the garland. Thread two or three extra beads at each end and knot securely.

SPOTTY & STRIPEY POMS

Learning to make spots and stripes is the first step towards more complex patterns. Practising these will help you master other projects. They are also a good way to get to grips with templates.

YOU WILL NEED

For the pompoms:
DK-weight acrylic yarn in the following colours: apricot, denim, saffron, white, aspen, fondant, lime, magenta

5.5cm (2⅛in) and 7cm (2¾in) diameter pompom makers

Scissors

TIP

To make a simple single spot pompom, follow the Liquorice Allsorts instructions on page 48, trim the finished pompom into a neat sphere. Once you have mastered the single spot, try making a multi-spot pompom following the template on page 44.

2

Wind 20 wraps of denim over apricot wedge. Then wind 30 wraps of apricot either side of denim.

1

For spot with outer ring, wind 40 wraps of apricot in centre of front maker in a wedge with widest part in centre. Wind 10 wraps of denim either side of wedge.

4

Complete pompom and remove it from maker. Trim pompom into a neat sphere.

3

Wind 40 wraps of apricot evenly to fill front maker. For a spot and ring on both sides, repeat steps 1–3 on back maker. For a plain side, fill back maker with wraps of apricot.

For basic single stripe,
1 wind 100 wraps of fondant over a 5.5cm (2⅛ in) maker, leaving far edges empty.

2 Wind 10 wraps of lime to fill empty spaces at both edges of maker.

3 Wind 20 wraps of lime across maker. Repeat on other half. Complete and remove from maker.

For beach ball stripe,
1 wind 80 wraps of magenta over a 7cm (2¾ in) maker, leaving far edges empty.

2 Wind 160 wraps of white, again, stopping just short of RHE and LHE.

3 Wind 20 wraps of saffron to fill spaces at edges, then 40 wraps over entire maker. Repeat on other half.

For crossed stripes,
1 wind 40 wraps of saffron evenly over one half of a 5.5cm (2⅛ in) maker.

2 Wind 30 wraps of saffron in centre in a wedge, keeping wedge 5 wraps wide and an even height.

3 Wind 40 wraps of lime each side of wedge. Repeat on other half. Complete and remove from maker.

SPOTS TEMPLATES

Spots like these are the foundation for projects such as the Sushi on page 57 and coconut roll Liquorice Allsort on page 48.

BASIC SINGLE SPOT
7cm (2¾ in) maker

40

80 40

40

MULTI SPOT
7cm (2¾ in) maker

50 20

50 44 30

20

50

SPOT WITH OUTER RING
7cm (2¾ in) maker

30

20

40

30

STRIPES TEMPLATES

Stripes like these are the foundation for projects, such as the Macapoms on page 47, the striped Liquorice Allsorts on page 51 and the cactus on page 55.

BASIC SINGLE STRIPE
5.5cm (2⅛in) maker

10
100
20
10

WIDE STRIPES
7cm (2¾in) maker

20
80
160
40
20

BEACH BALL STRIPE
7cm (2¾in) maker

50
100
100
100
100
50

CROSSED STRIPES
5.5cm (2⅛in) maker

40
40
30
40

MACAPOMS

Take what is possibly the most photogenic of all French pâtisserie and mix it with the cutest craft discipline and what do you get? The macapom, of course.

YOU WILL NEED

DK-weight acrylic yarn in the following colours: white, aspen, emperor, bluebell, fondant, cream, bright pink, soft peach, walnut, mocha, camel

5.5cm (2⅛in) diameter pompom maker

Scissors

TIP

For macarons with a speckled top, wrap two colours (the main colour and a yarn a couple of shades lighter or darker) across the centre of one half of the pompom maker as you are reaching the maker's capacity.

1

Starting at LHE, wrap 'filling' colour 40 times around one half of maker.

2

Wrap 'shell' colour 140 times around maker. Repeat on other half. Complete pompom and trim it into a neat sphere.

3

Flatten pompom between your palms. Holding it between your thumb and forefinger, trim the sides. Trim top and base shorter for a flatter shape.

4

Carefully trim 'filling' shorter than 'shell'. Continue trimming until you are happy with shape. Repeat with other colours for more macapoms.

LIQUORICE ALLSORTS

Liquorice Allsorts are in my Top Five Sweets Of All Time. The yellow or pink coconut rolls are my faves. Guess what?! You can buy packets of just those ones. They should be called Liquorice Sorts.

TO MAKE THE COCONUT ROLLS

YOU WILL NEED

DK-weight acrylic yarn in the following colours: white, black, fondant, citron, walnut, aster

3.5cm (1⅜ in) and 5.5cm (2⅛ in) diameter pompom makers

Scissors

TIP
To make the blue one, wind three shades of blue yarn together across a 3.5cm (1⅜ in) maker.

1
Wind 20 wraps of black at centre of one half of a 3.5cm (1⅜ in) maker, creating a wedge.

2
Wind 30 wraps of citron (or fondant) on both sides of black wedge.

3
Wind 30 wraps of citron evenly over entire maker. Fill other half of maker with citron. Complete and remove from maker.

4
With black spot top and bottom, trim pompom into a neat round, then trim top and base into a slightly flatter shape.

CONTINUED...

TO MAKE THE PRETTY STRIPEY ALLSORT

The most common of the Allsorts family, this three-layer delicacy comes in various colourways but always with a centre liquorice stripe.

1

Wind 60 wraps of white on a 3.5cm (1⅜ in) maker, leaving far edges empty. Wind 30 wraps of black, filling gaps at edges.

2

Repeat on other half of maker using walnut (or fondant or aster) and black. Complete and remove from maker.

3

Flatten pompom with white and walnut top and bottom. Trim sides into a square. Trim top and base into a flatter shape.

TO MAKE THE SUPER-SIZE ALLSORT

You do not get many of these Allsorts per pack, but it is the sweetie that everyone wants as it is simply massive.

1

Wind 75 wraps of white on a 5.5cm (2⅛ in) maker, stopping before both edges. Wind 50 wraps of black, filling half of empty gaps at both edges.

2

Wind 30 wraps of fondant over black, filling in rest of empty spaces on both sides. Repeat on other half of maker. Complete and remove from maker.

3

Flatten pompom with white top and bottom. Trim sides into a square. Trim top and base into a flatter shape.

CACTI

These cacti pompoms are a lot less prickly than their living counterparts.

YOU WILL NEED

DK-weight acrylic yarn in the following colours: meadow, saffron, green, lime

3.5cm (1⅜ in), 5.5cm (2⅛ in) and 7cm (2¾ in) diameter pompom makers

Scissors

Small plant pot

1

For mottled cactus, wind 15 wraps of meadow over right half of 5.5cm (2⅛ in) front maker. Wind 2 wraps of saffron around centre and trim back yarn ends.

2

Wind wraps of meadow over left half. Wind meadow back and forth, interspersed with 2 wraps of saffron at random intervals, to fill maker.

3

Repeat steps 1–2 on back maker. Complete pompom and remove it from maker. Repeat all steps using a 3.5cm (1⅜ in) maker to make three smaller pompoms.

4

Roughly trim larger pompom into an oval with a flat base. Trim the smaller pompoms with flat bases. Using glue gun, fix mini-poms to main pompom body.

CONTINUED...

If you want your cactus to flower, make some tiny pink pompoms using the fork method (page 7). Trim them and then stick them to the top of your main cactus with a glue gun.

3

Continue in alternate layers as follows: 80 wraps green, 50 wraps lime, 80 wraps green, 50 wraps lime, 40 wraps green.

6

Work around pompom, trimming back each green section. If preferred, add small pink flowers to cactus (see left). Place in a suitable small plant pot and display.

2

Wind 50 wraps of lime to cover evenly the previous green layer.

5

Carefully separate the lime and the green stripes. Trim back some of green to make lime strands stand out like spines of a cactus.

1

For stripey cactus, wind 40 wraps of green over 7cm (2¾ in) front maker.

4

Repeat steps 1–3 on back maker. Complete pompom and remove it from maker. With stripes vertical, roughly trim into a flat base, keeping yarn strands long on rest of pompom.

SUSHI

How cute is this pompom sushi? From a distance it's fairly hard to tell it's not real… although it quickly becomes obvious when you try and take a bite.

DK-weight acrylic yarn in the following colours:
shrimp, white, cream, green, greengage, jaffa, peach, saffron

3.5cm (1⅜in) and 5.5cm (2⅛in) diameter pompom makers

Scissors

1

For salmon maki rolls, wind 10 wraps of shrimp in centre of 3.5cm (1⅜in) front maker.

2

Wind 5 wraps of cream and white together either side of shrimp, then 5 wraps over shrimp.

3

Wind 35 wraps of green over maker. Repeat steps 1–3 on back maker. Complete using strands of shrimp to tie it together. Remove from maker.

To make egg maki rolls, follow the instructions for the salmon maki rolls but use saffron for the centre instead of shrimp. For cucumber maki rolls, use greengage for the centre.

4

Holding pompom around green centre, trim white and shrimp side flat. Repeat on opposite side. Trim green into a cylindrical shape.

1

For California rolls, wind 10 wraps of greengage just off centre of a 5.5cm (2⅛ in) maker.

2

Wind 15 wraps of peach to left of greengage, then 5 wraps of shrimp to left of peach.

3

Wind 5 wraps of green either side of previous layer, then 10 wraps of green over previous layer.

4

Wind 10 wraps of white and cream each side of green, leaving far edges empty, then 45 across maker.

5

Wind a further 5 wraps of cream and white to cover any visible green.

6

Wind 40 wraps of shrimp and jaffa together over maker filling empty areas at edges of maker.

7

Repeat steps 1–6 on other half. Complete with strands of peach to tie pompom. Remove from maker.

8

Holding pompom around orange centre, trim cream, white and green side flat. Repeat on opposite side.

9

Trim orange centre into a cylindrical shape. Keep trimming until you are happy with the shape.

NICE PEAR

This pompom pear is unbelievably tactile. It looks best when trimmed hard, so do not be afraid to go at it with the scissors.

YOU WILL NEED

DK-weight acrylic yarn in the following colours:
pomegranate, shrimp, meadow, lime, walnut

7cm (2¾ in) and 9cm (3½ in) diameter pompom makers

Scissors

Glue gun

1

For lower part, using a 9cm (3½ in) maker, wind 100 wraps of pomegranate in a wedge, leaving one quarter of maker empty at both RHE and LHE.

2

Wind 20 wraps of pomegranate and shrimp together over previous layer, covering wedge.

3

Wind 30 wraps of shrimp and meadow together over previous layer.

4

Wind 15 wraps of shrimp, meadow and lime together over previous layer.

CONTINUED...

5

Wind 20 wraps of meadow and lime to fill gaps at each edge, then 50 of meadow and lime to fill maker.

6

To finish, fill other half of maker with meadow and lime. Complete pompom and remove it from maker.

7

For top, using a 7cm (2¾in) maker, wind 40 wraps of shrimp, meadow and lime across three quarters.

8

Fill maker with 120 wraps of meadow and lime. To finish, fill other half of maker with meadow and lime.

9

Complete pompom using three strands of walnut to tie it together. Remove it from maker.

10

Trim flat base of smaller and top and base of larger pompom. Fix together, matching speckled areas.

11

Trim the pompoms into a neat pear shape. Keep trimming until you are happy with the shape.

12

For the stalk, plait the three walnut strands together for 3–4cm (1¼–1½in). Knot and trim.

CUPCAKES

Everybody loves a cupcake – and if bakings not your thing then these adorable cupcake pompoms are ideal.

DK-weight acrylic yarn in the following colours: white, glittery white, walnut, lipstick red, citron, fondant, aspen

3.5cm (1⅜ in) and 9cm (3½ in) diameter pompom makers

Scissors

Darning needle

TIP

Make fake candles using a cut down paper straw and some gold paper or streamer. Don't be tempted to use real candles!

1

For a cherry cupcake, on one half of a 9cm (3½ in) maker wind 350 wraps of walnut yarn (or till the maker half is two thirds full).

2

Then wind 50 wraps of white and glittery white yarn making 100 wraps in total.

3

Fill the other half of the maker with the white and glittery white yarn mix.

4

Complete the pompom using two strands of walnut to tie it together. Remove it from maker. Do not trim away the long walnut tails.

CONTINUED...

7

For the cherry, make a small lipstick red pompom with a 3.5cm (1⅜in) maker. Trim and cut off the long tails.

6

Shape the top half of the cupcake, so the icing looks like it is overflowing the cake base.

5

Starting with the base of the cupcake, carefully trim it into a slight conical shape with a flat bottom.

10

Trim away the excess yarn at the stalk and any stray strands you may spot.

9

Nestle the cherry into the icing, then plait the yarn tails together to create a short stalk.

8

Thread the long walnut yarn tails onto a needle and insert through the centre of the cherry pompom.

3

Fill the rest of the maker with fondant yarn, then finish off and trim pompom as before.

2

Wind 10 wraps of walnut, aspen, citron, fondant, lipstick red and white yarn around the centre of the other half maker.

1

For a sprinkles cupcake, fill one half of the maker with walnut then fondant yarn as before.

ICE CREAM CONES

They may not taste as good as the real thing, but there's no chance of these little beauties melting in the sunshine.

YOU WILL NEED

DK-weight acrylic yarn in the following colours:
red, cream, white, bright pink, cream, biscuit

7cm (2¾in) diameter pompom maker

Scissors

Glue gun

TO MAKE THE CONE

1

Wind 140 wraps of cream and biscuit together over a 7cm (2¾ in) maker to make a two-tone pompom, oval in shape.

2

Roughly trim pompom at one narrow end to make a flat surface.

3

Neatly trim rest of pompom into a pointed cone shape.

4

Trim a slight indent in top of flat surface for ice cream scoop to sit inside.

TIP

Add choc chips to a scoop by winding scattered blocks of brown yarn into a mint green pompom. Follow the instructions for the cactus on page 52 for extra help.

CONTINUED...

TO MAKE THE RASPBERRY RIPPLE SCOOP

1

For raspberry, wind 10 wraps of red one quarter of way from RHE.

2

For ripple, wind 3 wraps of red, bright pink and white together next to red.

3

Wind 10 wraps of bright pink and white together over right half.

4

Wind 50 wraps of white back and forth over entire maker.

5

Repeat steps 1–4, winding 10 wraps of red in a different position.

6

For a random ripple, vary number of wraps of each colour wound together.

7

Continue repeating steps to fill maker, wrapping white between ripples.

8

Repeat steps 1–7 on other half of maker. Complete and remove it from maker.

9

Trim pompom with base flat to sit on cone. Using a glue gun, fix scoop to cone.

FLORAL POMPOMS

These delicate flowers are a perfect example of how the symmetry of pompom making works. They look impressive, but are actually not that tricky. The flower shape forms naturally as you wind the yarn.

YOU WILL NEED

DK-weight acrylic yarn in the following colours:
emperor, shrimp, sage, cream, peach

9cm (3½ in) diameter pompom maker

Scissors

1

Wind 10 wraps of emperor in a wedge in centre of front maker.

2

Wind 12 wraps of emperor and peach together over wedge.

3

Wind 10 wraps of shrimp next to wedge on left.

4

Wind 80 wraps of shrimp back and forth across maker in a wedge with widest part towards RHE and leaving a gap at RHE.

5

Wind 20 wraps of sage to fill gap at RHE.

7

Wind 20 wraps of peach to cover but NOT fill gap at LHE.

10

Wind 20 wraps of sage over point where peach and shrimp meet on previous layer.

6

Wind 50 wraps of shrimp at LHE, leaving a gap at LHE.

9

Wind 20 wraps of sage to fill remaining empty gap at LHE.

13

If preferred, trim flower into a neat round. Keep trimming until you are happy with shape.

8

Wind 30 wraps of peach over left third of maker, leaving a small gap at LHE.

12

Floral pompoms look gorgeous neatly trimmed, but also have a certain charm left untrimmed.

11

Wind 200 wraps of cream to fill maker. Fill back maker with cream. Complete pompom.

LOVE HEARTS

A love heart pompom is the perfect gift for a loved one. When making the 'heart inside' pompom, keep picturing the shape of a heart as you wind the yarn and you will find it easier to build up the heart shape within the pompom.

DK-weight acrylic yarn in the following colours:
light blue, dark blue, red

7cm (2¾in) diameter pompom maker

Scissors

TIP

When trimming, to make a neater heart shape, keep brushing the yarn in different directions and trim where necessary.

TO MAKE THE HEART-SHAPED POMPOM

1

Make a pompom in the usual way. Complete and remove from maker, but do not trim it into a round.

2

Holding yarn tails in one hand, trim pompom into a conical shape to make bottom point of heart.

3

Cut a V-shaped groove in centre of upper half to make the top of heart.

4

Trim each side into a heart shape. Start at side then work round from front to back, trimming little bits.

CONTINUED...

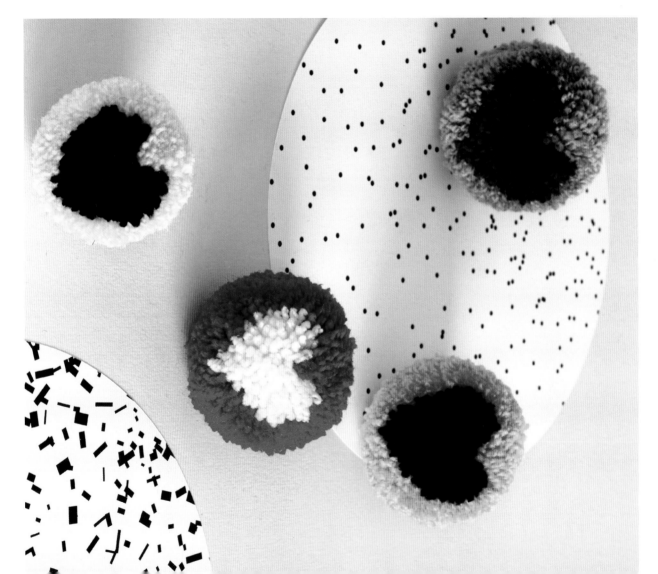

TO MAKE THE HEART-INSIDE POMPOM

1

For 'V' shape, wind 12 wraps of dark blue, working one third in towards LHE. Make sure each strand lies flat and does not overlap.

2

Wind 8 wraps to right, then wind 6 wraps to left to build a wedge with widest part at LHE. Repeat this four times.

3

Wind 20 wraps of red, overlapping first 4 wraps of blue and working towards RHE, finishing one quarter in from RHE.

4

Wind 10 wraps of red back to left, starting 2 wraps in from previous layer. Then wind 50 wraps back and forth decreasing width of area to build a wedge with widest part at top.

5

Wind 60 wraps of blue back and forth starting in centre and working to RHE, filling right side of maker evenly. Wind 100 wraps of blue to fill entire maker. To finish, fill other half of maker with blue.

6

Complete and remove from maker. Trim pompom into a neat round. Keep trimming until you are happy with the shape. The harder you trim, the clearer the heart shape becomes.

EMOJI POMPOMS

This friendly crew of smiley pompoms are all made in a similar way. Once you get the hang of how faces are created in pompom world, you can make a whole set of emojis… maybe even the smiley poop.

TO MAKE THE SMILEY FACE EMOJI

1

For smile, one third in from RHE, wind 5 wraps of black and citron next to each other. This keeps smile straight when cutting open pompom.

2

For chin, wind 60 wraps of citron back and forth from RHE, stopping at black. If citron ends higher, wind a couple more wraps of black until level.

3

Wind 60 wraps of citron back and forth from LHE, stopping at black, filling in empty part of maker.

4

For eyes, wind 8 wraps of black over citron to left of mouth.

CONTINUED…

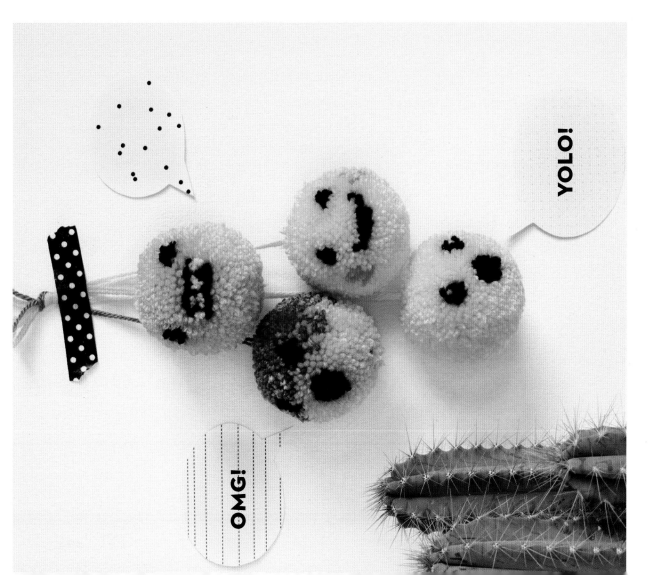

EMOJI TEMPLATES

SMILEY EMOJI

Follow this diagram for the front half of the Smiley Emoji. For the back half, wind wraps of citron yarn over the maker until full. Complete the pompom and remove from the maker.

GRINNING EMOJI

Follow this diagram for the front half of the Grinning Emoji. For the back half, wind wraps of citron yarn over the maker until full. Complete the pompom and remove from the maker.

SURPRISED EMOJI

Follow this diagram for the front half of the Surprised Emoji. For the back half, fill the maker with citron yarn. Thread a darning needle with white and sew highlights into the pupils.

FEARFUL EMOJI

Follow this diagram for the front half of the Fearful Emoji. For the back half, from RHE to LHE, wind: 100 citron, 40 citron and turquoise, 80 turquoise. Match colour changes on front and back.

7

Wind 10 wraps of fondant in centre of maker. Then wind 50 wraps of citron to fill maker evenly.

6

Wind 30 wraps of citron over right half of maker, including mouth and chin.

9

Trim the smiley face into a neat round. Keep trimming until you are happy with the shape. These emoji faces look best when neat and tidy.

TIP

By moving around individual strands of coloured yarn, you can really affect the expression of these little characters. Use either a needle or tiny scissors to position the strands of yarn, then trim.

5

Wind 80 wraps of citron over left half of maker, including eyes.

8

To finish, fill back maker with citron. Complete and remove from maker.

DIA DE MUERTOS SKULL

A perfect pompom to make for a Day of the Dead celebration or Hallowe'en event. Although he's not remotely scary.

DK-weight acrylic yarn in the following colours:
white, black, turquoise, red, yellow, metallic gold, bright pink

Scissors

9cm (3½ in) diameter pompom maker

1

For nose, wind 10 wraps of black in a wedge from centre towards RHE. Wind 10 wraps of white next to black. For teeth, wind 10 wraps of black and white parallel, 2 wraps wide.

2

For chin, at RHE of maker, wind 20 wraps of turquoise and red together in a wedge with widest part at edge of maker.

3

Wind 20 wraps of white between chin and teeth. Wind 30 wraps of white to left of nose. Wind 10 wraps of yellow over white towards LHE. Wind 10 wraps of white until even.

4

For eye sockets, wind 60 wraps of gold, starting a couple of wraps down from top of yellow, finishing a couple of wraps up from nose.

CONTINUED...

5

Wind 15 wraps of turquoise over gold, starting and finishing a couple of wraps in from edges of gold. Then wind 10 wraps of black in centre of turquoise.

6

Wind 15 wraps of turquoise over black, then wind 60 wraps of gold over turquoise.

7

To complete eye socket, wind 10 wraps of yellow over gold. At LHE of maker wind 12 wraps of bright pink and red leaving a gap to yellow. Fill gap with 10 wraps of white.

8

Fill maker with white. There is already more yarn at LHE of maker due to the eye sockets; this helps to give a natural skull shape.

9

To complete pompom, fill other half of maker with white. Complete and remove it from maker.

10

Trim the skull so it is naturally pointy towards chin, but bulbous at crown. Keep trimming until you are happy with the shape.

POMPOMERANIAN

If someone is going to breed a dog so small and cute that it can fit in a teacup – and name it a Pomeranian – it would simply be rude not to recreate one made from pompoms.

YOU WILL NEED

DK-weight acrylic yarn in the following colours:
white, peach, fondant, walnut, black, stone, parchment, cream

7cm (2¾ in) and 9cm (3½ in) diameter pompom makers

Scissors

Glue gun

Darning needle

TIP
Plait together several strands of contrast colour yarn to make a collar for your pompomeranian.

1
For nose, from centre towards RHE, wind 10 wraps of walnut in a wedge with widest part at centre. For tongue, wind 6 wraps of peach and fondant together to right of walnut.

2
For muzzle, wind 50 wraps of white and cream over right half in a wedge with widest part at centre. Stop before RHE. Wind 60 wraps of parchment over left half. Stop before LHE.

3
For eyes, wind 20 wraps of black at centre where cream and parchment meet, winding towards LHE for 4 wraps and then back and forth.

4
Wind 30 wraps of parchment to cover black eyes. Wind 90 wraps of parchment in a wedge over parchment and half of cream muzzle.

5

Wind 60 wraps of stone evenly over empty space at RHE and cream muzzle, stopping at parchment.

6

Wind 140 wraps of stone over maker, including space at LHE. Fill other half with stone. Complete pompom.

7

Trim face until features become clear. Leave yarn for muzzle and nose longer than eyes and forehead.

8

Trim back of head, leaving yarn longer for ears. Keep trimming until you are happy with the shape.

9

Add highlight to eyes by sewing a length of white yarn through each pupil, then trim.

10

For body, wind 110 wraps of cream and white from LHE to RHE of maker.

11

Wind 70 wraps of stone over cream and white. Fill other half with stone. Complete pompom.

12

Trim body base flat and chest slightly shorter than haunches and back. Using a glue gun, fix head to body.

HEY, BIRDIE

A fluffy little baby birdie who just wants someone to love him.

DK-weight acrylic yarn in the following colours:

lemon, saffron, aspen, white, walnut, black, aster, turquoise

7cm (2¾in) and 9cm (3½in) diameter pompom makers

Scissors

Glue gun

TIP

Only got grey, black and white yarn in your stash? Don't worry. Those shades make the most perfect baby penguin.

1

For tummy, starting at LHE, wind 16 wraps of lemon towards centre. Wind 8 wraps of lemon and saffron together at centre. Wind 16 wraps of saffron, finishing at RHE.

2

Working back towards LHE, wind 14 wraps of saffron, 8 wraps of lemon and saffron together, then 11 wraps of lemon, finishing just short of LHE.

3

Working towards RHE, wind 11 wraps of lemon, 10 wraps of lemon and saffron, then 60 wraps of saffron in a wedge with widest part at RHE.

4

Wind a further 7 wraps of lemon and saffron together and 8 wraps of lemon, finishing at LHE. Side on, there is more yarn at bottom than top.

CONTINUED...

5

From LHE, wind: 40 aspen, 50 aster, 30 turquoise. On other half, wind: 80 aspen, 80 aster, 70 turquoise.

6

For beak, starting just off centre, wind 20 wraps of walnut in a wedge with widest part towards LHE.

7

Wind 80 wraps of lemon from RHE to beyond beak. Wind 10 wraps of lemon and aspen, then 50 aspen.

8

Wind 40 wraps of white from beak to third in LHE. Wind 10 wraps of black in centre, 3 wraps wide.

9

Wind 40 wraps of white over previous white layer. Wind 90 wraps of lemon over right half of maker.

10

Wind 10 wraps of lemon and aspen over remaining visible white. Wind 60 wraps of aspen at LHE.

11

On other half, wind: 230 aster and aspen. From RHE, wind: 40 lemon, 10 aspen and lemon, 15 aspen.

12

Complete pompoms. Trim body base and top flat, so head nestles in place. Trim breast shorter than wings.

13

Trim face, leaving beak and back. Trim head base flat. Trim beak into point. Using glue gun, fix head to body.

THANK YOU...

Firstly, a huge thank you to both Stylecraft and LoveCrafts for providing balls and balls and balls of yarn.

To everyone who I have taught how to make a pompom over the past year or so – it was great to see so many people revisiting their childhood memories and gasping in wonder at the advancements in pompom technology!

To the wonderful Jo for her fantastic photography and for going above and beyond the call of pompom duty allowing us to use her home as a location and her ironing board as a desk!

To all the usual suspects... Mum, Dad, Jo, Ian, Oliver and Elliot (both super-skilled pompom makers whose poms have made the cover of this book), Jake, Kirsty and Laura, Lottie and Hannah – for letting us move every single piece of furniture in her living room to get the shots just right!

WANT MORE?

If you need even more pompoms in your life then I have an online Domestika course showing you how to make a pompom wreath with simple video tutorials. It uses many of the techniques in this book plus lots of tips for perfect pompoms. Visit Domestika.com and search pompoms or Christine Leech for more information.

You can also find many more tutorials on my instagram @sewyeah or at my website sewyeahsocialclub.com

HERE'S TO WORLD POMINATION!

stylecraftyarns.co.uk: Purveyors of the best yarn for making pompoms.

lovecrafts.com: This website has everything you need to get pompooning, from yarn galore to haberdashery bits 'n' bobs and a variety of pompom makers.

hobbycraft.co.uk: Basically your go-to store for all things crafty.

tigerstores.co.uk: Tiger have a great set of pompom makers in a variety of sizes.